BECOME YOUR BEST

MASTERING CONFIDENCE
THROUGH
6 PHASES OF QUOTES & NOTES

This book is for anyone looking to master their confidence. This book is not just for adults. This book is not just for youth. This book is not just for business people, those in relationships, or sports athletes. This book is for anyone looking to master their confidence.

Written by:
Chris P Austin

Edited by:
Lynn Flanagan & Palmer McDonald

Printed in the United States of America

First Printing Edition, 2020

ISBN 978-0-9976371-0-6 (PB)
ISBN 978-0-9976371-3-7 (eBook)
ISBN 978-0-9976371-4-4 (Audio)

FOREWARD

by C.J. Watson
10 year NBA veteran

Confidence is key! That is what my dad told me when I was younger. Once it is established you can't take it away. Confidence is all you need to play this game and in the game of life. It can and will take you to levels you never imagined. There's one key ingredient that all successful people have, and confidence is at the core of that success. Confidence is the attribute that most people would like to possess because it gives you the skills and coping methods to handle setbacks and failure.

I met Chris randomly just scrolling on Instagram one day, browsing for coaching for my daughter. Seeing that he was an athlete previously and was successful sparked my interest, being that I was an athlete, also. It meant he knew about the ups and downs that come with being an athlete, and then to be able to experience those things and teach others is a testament to his character, knowledge and expertise. The experience ended up being more than my family had imagined. Chris not only teaches the fundamentals of his process, but also helps condition the mind and body, while instilling confidence and focus into his clients. While there aren't many coaches in our area with his resume, we travel to wherever he is to get the teaching and coaching we need to be able to compete at a high level.

This book will help you master the mental aspect you need to be confident, get all the tools you need to master your confidence, and to become the best version of yourself.

No matter what walk of life you're embarking on, you have to be confident in your abilities whether it be in the boardroom or on the court. Set the bar high and aim high!

DEDICATION

This book is dedicated to the first CPA Facility and every partner, family member, client, friend, and Young Lion who helped make it possible.

TABLE OF CONTENTS

Your Confidence
is worth
investing in.

— CHRIS P AUSTIN —

PHASE 1

AWARENESS

"If you aren't in the position you want
to be in on the
team/business/relationship,
have a transparent conversation
with the leader...
and then you become a leader."

AWARENESS

"Remember the power of believing in
yourself."

AWARENESS

"Going for it will give you the best
opportunity to be successful.
If you don't go for it, you, for sure,
won't be successful."

AWARENESS

"The most successful people in the
world are those who understand the
importance of happiness... real
happiness.
Happiness is success."

AWARENESS

"At a high level, most have talent and ability and experience.
What separates success and happiness is mentality."

AWARENESS

"You don't have to be born a champion to become a champion."

AWARENESS

"The most we've ever seen someone learn, is when they were willing."

AWARENESS

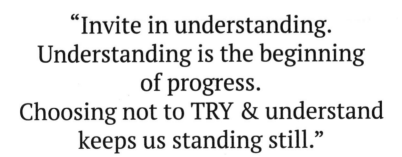

"Invite in understanding.
Understanding is the beginning
of progress.
Choosing not to TRY & understand
keeps us standing still."

AWARENESS

"The best way to make it better begins
with a conversation. However,
it doesn't end with a conversation.
Actions speak."

AWARENESS

"There are many ways to become great,
yet very few ways to make the decision."

AWARENESS

"Becoming great at your craft requires so much little detail in the shadows. These current shadows can be used."

AWARENESS

"Happiness will be found when hard work and time spent meet one another. Hard work + Time spent."

AWARENESS

"Your life will be what you work for.
Dust will settle on what you were born
with, and then the work...
It's never too early or too late
to learn that."

AWARENESS

"Stacking chips is the first thing you
do. In standard terms that means:
SAVE FIRST. The next questions are
"save what?" and "save how?"

AWARENESS

"Don't be fooled... the fastest way to
the top is STILL the stairs."

AWARENESS

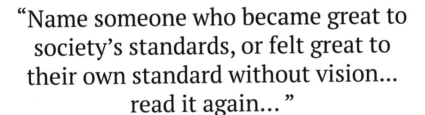

"Name someone who became great to
society's standards, or felt great to
their own standard without vision...
read it again... "

AWARENESS

"If you want more happiness, have a relationship with the work. Work and progress invite confidence."

AWARENESS

"Happiness should come before money."

AWARENESS

"Don't discount the power of setting goals. It can change your life."

AWARENESS

"The world has so few leaders.
Look around, see if that's accurate.
Then use it as an opportunity
to step up."

AWARENESS

"If it's what YOU want to do, then you're on the right track. Keep going."

AWARENESS

"Mistakes are real and important. Mistake response is real and more important."

AWARENESS

"You responding with how bad you
are at something is the fastest way to
NOT improve.
Confidence breeds results."

AWARENESS

"If you've got goals to reach...
Start today."

AWARENESS

"If you say you want to start, then you better go ahead and start..."

AWARENESS

"This is the right time and place to start your upward trajectory to reach as high as is possible for you."

AWARENESS

"There are consequences to having confidence. Accept the consequences."

AWARENESS

"Belief can be trained."

AWARENESS

"Are there those out there who
embrace what is difficult?"

AWARENESS

"Develop your opinion based on your
own experiences; today and every day."

AWARENESS

"Let's get a little bit better today."

AWARENESS

"Life will continue to improve. It begins between the ears."

AWARENESS

"Mentality over Age."

AWARENESS

PHASE 2

CONFIDENCE
COMES FROM ME

"Confidence is what separates good from great, the belief in yourself."

CONFIDENCE COMES FROM ME

"Mentality is something that can be taught. And having a strong confidence and understanding of how you get yourself to that place creates happiness for your life."

CONFIDENCE COMES FROM ME

"Shoot your shot. Worst case... you're in the same position you're in now: without."

CONFIDENCE COMES FROM ME

"Don't compare yourself to others. You will never be them, and they will never be you."

CONFIDENCE COMES FROM ME

"If you aren't believing in you...
all the technical and hands-on training
will be a waste.
Success begins with believing in you."

CONFIDENCE COMES FROM ME

"Becoming your own biggest fan will
lead you to more happiness much faster.
Then you'll really be able to help others."

CONFIDENCE COMES FROM ME

"Taking stress away from your life begins with taking away the value of outside opinions of yourself."

CONFIDENCE COMES FROM ME

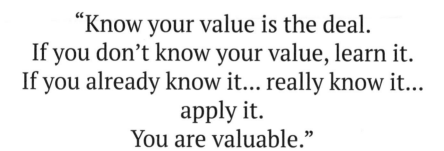

"Know your value is the deal.
If you don't know your value, learn it.
If you already know it... really know it...
apply it.
You are valuable."

CONFIDENCE COMES FROM ME

"Be unconcerned about what the world thinks. Be concerned with what makes you improve... and then what helps others around you improve."

CONFIDENCE COMES FROM ME

"Becoming your best will be decided by you. Others' opinions slow the process. You go ahead and choose."

CONFIDENCE COMES FROM ME

"Quit turning your neck to find YOUR success.
The mirror is in front of you."

CONFIDENCE COMES FROM ME

"Your opinion about you is primary and most important. Make it a good one."

CONFIDENCE COMES FROM ME

"The importance of understanding what is beautiful about you cannot be overstated."

CONFIDENCE COMES FROM ME

"Know what's valuable about yourself... then add."

CONFIDENCE COMES FROM ME

"Your best is determined by doing all you can with what YOU have. Although others can help, your best isn't determined by other people."

CONFIDENCE COMES FROM ME

"Tell yourself... that you believe in yourself. You'll be closer."

CONFIDENCE COMES FROM ME

"Tell yourself three GOOD and very different things about yourself today. Lather. Rinse. Repeat."

CONFIDENCE COMES FROM ME

"Learn as quickly as possible, that there is only one person who can REALLY tell you that you're good or not good."

CONFIDENCE COMES FROM ME

"If you want to be a beast, quit telling yourself you're a weenie."

CONFIDENCE COMES FROM ME

"You are in charge of where you get to. Enjoy that responsibility and embrace it."

CONFIDENCE COMES FROM ME

"It can be as simple as telling yourself YOU CAN DO IT."

CONFIDENCE COMES FROM ME

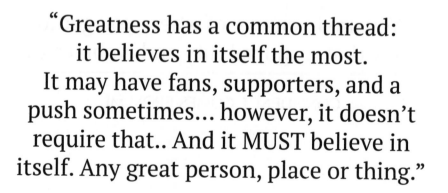

"Greatness has a common thread:
it believes in itself the most.
It may have fans, supporters, and a
push sometimes... however, it doesn't
require that.. And it MUST believe in
itself. Any great person, place or thing."

CONFIDENCE COMES FROM ME

"How special you are isn't determined by your parents or your kids. You be the show."

CONFIDENCE COMES FROM ME

"That which you seek, should show attraction back to you, in order for it to become a thing. Business, crafts, sports, relationships, etc..."

CONFIDENCE COMES FROM ME

"The world isn't waiting for you to be ready. Just decide you're ready."

CONFIDENCE COMES FROM ME

"We are in control of how we respond... to all things verbal, emotional, and mental."

CONFIDENCE COMES FROM ME

"Notice yourself, and you won't require someone else's attention."

CONFIDENCE COMES FROM ME

"Being great does require gaining confidence from someone. That someone would be you..."

CONFIDENCE COMES FROM ME

"Yourself is what YOU CHOOSE...
it's not something you were born and
destined to be... or someone you were
raised to be... WHO YOU ARE
is a choice of yours."

CONFIDENCE COMES FROM ME

"Your best chance of getting seen is
being the first to believe in your vision."

CONFIDENCE COMES FROM ME

"Believe in your ability to create great."

CONFIDENCE COMES FROM ME

"If it wasn't for the struggle then you wouldn't be you."

CONFIDENCE COMES FROM ME

"Confidence is in our control."

CONFIDENCE COMES FROM ME

PHASE 3

ADDING TO MYSELF

"The same person you see in your head is the same person you are. Those persons can be developed."

ADDING TO MYSELF

"Break down the barriers of potential and unlock the stratosphere of progress."

ADDING TO MYSELF

"People want to connect with whoever or whatever is going to be their bridge... without realizing that they, themselves, are the bridge."

ADDING TO MYSELF

"Saving money isn't just for when you're making a relatively large amount of money. Saving a percentage is for always."

ADDING TO MYSELF

"Working out your body is a portion of becoming your best."

ADDING TO MYSELF

"Being vocal or assertive or in front isn't something you're born with or a privilege at birth. It's a decision you make on a daily basis."

ADDING TO MYSELF

"Be multifaceted and you'll have multiple opportunities."

ADDING TO MYSELF

"No matter your childhood experience, everyone can find lessons in their upbringing... and current life."

ADDING TO MYSELF

"Competition is how to get to a new level.
Competition with self is the best kind."

ADDING TO MYSELF

"Become great at controlling
the pace of your life.
Then the world's pace won't
matter much."

ADDING TO MYSELF

"Being willing to work is what gets you
to the next level.
Sitting back and waiting is rare
to get results. Go get it!"

ADDING TO MYSELF

"Working out isn't a waste of time.
It's time well spent.
Find your time and workout your body.
Workout your mind."

ADDING TO MYSELF

"Competing against others will give you gains. Competing against yourself will give you greater gains."

ADDING TO MYSELF

"Youth & adults: look to handle your own responsibilities. More confidence comes with doing your own work."

ADDING TO MYSELF

"The WHOLE deal is challenge-solving.
Learn to solve challenges and
you'll really enjoy your life.
Make this day what you want it to be."

ADDING TO MYSELF

"Invite less "seeing what others can do"
into your stuff. Invite more "seeing
what I (you) will do"."

ADDING TO MYSELF

"The number one way to gain experience is to travel. Outside of your house, outside of your city, outside of your state/country, outside of that COMFORT!"

ADDING TO MYSELF

"The grind isn't waiting for you to have more energy. Helping yourself and others become as good as possible can give you energy."

ADDING TO MYSELF

"If you want to get to a new level,
you'll have to be alright with
the temporary dip, before
you shoot it through the roof."

ADDING TO MYSELF

"If you feel like you're at the top... build
some new floors at your building."

ADDING TO MYSELF

"Any person can have an ideal
environment. Being able to
exist->succeed->thrive in ANY
environment is what makes
full-time value."

ADDING TO MYSELF

"Get in the figurative kitchen and bake
your dreams into reality."

ADDING TO MYSELF

"Wake up lookin' to make a life better and more meaningful... start with your own, and then branch."

ADDING TO MYSELF

"If you are going to talk,
talk about what you're going to do,
rather than what you're
NOT going to do. Serves more purpose."

ADDING TO MYSELF

"Quit doing stuff for the money and you'll be closer to the happiness you seek."

ADDING TO MYSELF

"Tomorrow I will become greater than I was today... at life."

ADDING TO MYSELF

"Becoming a champion is at
the tips of your fingers and lips,
you just have to start."

ADDING TO MYSELF

"Each (fill in) can be great.
We have to make it reality.
Like anything worth having."

ADDING TO MYSELF

"Get in some gratitude before
you get your day going.
However things are, they could be worse.
And however things are,
you can make them even better."

ADDING TO MYSELF

"End up where you are on purpose.
Don't let it be an accident."

ADDING TO MYSELF

PHASE 4

URGENCY
IDEOLOGY

"The time is now.
Waiting is a waste of time."

URGENCY IDEOLOGY

"Later is not the best time
to get it done. Now..."

URGENCY IDEOLOGY

"The time to jump on the train isn't later... the train is leaving."

URGENCY IDEOLOGY

"Waiting for the right time is allowing the right time to pass you by. The right time is right now."

URGENCY IDEOLOGY

"The want won't ever be stronger than the need. Pursue what you need in order to be successful. I'm on that tip."

URGENCY IDEOLOGY

"Trying your hardest IS enough... if it's really your hardest."

URGENCY IDEOLOGY

"Having the discipline to receive
and NOT spend right away
is the start of feeling solid financially.
Receive and assess."

URGENCY IDEOLOGY

"Go ahead and reach for the top of the
mountain... realize you aren't there...
keep going."

URGENCY IDEOLOGY

"Because the world is different doesn't mean you can't still get to your goals. This is where those who practice mental toughness rise up."

URGENCY IDEOLOGY

"If you don't do it, there is less of a guarantee that it gets done. So Nike... just do it."

URGENCY IDEOLOGY

"Go for it today.
You won't get this day back."

URGENCY IDEOLOGY

"Tomorrow isn't the day to work
at what you want.
Today is the day to go get it."

URGENCY IDEOLOGY

"Challenge your limits, and take chances.
The alternative is having no chance..."

URGENCY IDEOLOGY

―――――――――――――∞―――――――――――――

"It's unlikely you'll maximize your
potential by hedging your bets.
If you wait to get out of your first thing,
while you get your next thing setup...
someone is likely passing you up.
Just go now!"

URGENCY IDEOLOGY

"To have great influence requires
great sacrifice.
So decide to enjoy that challenge."

URGENCY IDEOLOGY

"Avoid being satisfied with the result.
Look for that satisfaction after the work.
Then you're going somewhere."

URGENCY IDEOLOGY

"If this life were your only chance... what would your goals be?"

URGENCY IDEOLOGY

"Treat the week like it's your only one. Go after what you want now! Next week is too late."

URGENCY IDEOLOGY

"It's not always going to be perfect."

URGENCY IDEOLOGY

"If today were the first... If today were the last... What would you do?"

URGENCY IDEOLOGY

PHASE 5

ADDING TO OTHERS

"Creating opportunities for others
will create opportunities for yourself."

ADDING TO OTHERS

"A starting point is surrounding yourself
with those who desire
upward and forward movement.
Success CAN begin alone...
it only grows with community, though."

ADDING TO OTHERS

"Show them you care about their
progress as much as they do."

ADDING TO OTHERS

"What creates is our ability to raise
the level of ourselves and others.
What tears down is trying to shove
down others for our gain."

ADDING TO OTHERS

"Good leaders don't pick a side to
support. The best leaders help
all parties understand."

ADDING TO OTHERS

"Step One: make yourself as good as
you can today. Step Two: help others get
as good as they can. The best way
to help another is to show the demo...
do it yourself."

ADDING TO OTHERS

"You don't have to deal with anyone
who you feel is acting wild.
Yet, you should make an effort to create
community."

ADDING TO OTHERS

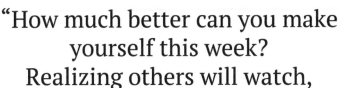

"How much better can you make
yourself this week?
Realizing others will watch,
and follow suit."

ADDING TO OTHERS

"Make someone else smile today. Stuff is contagious."

ADDING TO OTHERS

"Keep the hard workers around you, then embrace the competition."

ADDING TO OTHERS

"The most productive way to help others
is by showing how, rather than doing for."

ADDING TO OTHERS

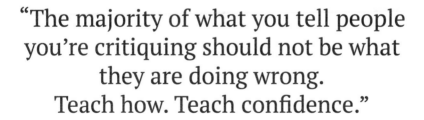

"The majority of what you tell people
you're critiquing should not be what
they are doing wrong.
Teach how. Teach confidence."

ADDING TO OTHERS

"Motivate into momentum."

ADDING TO OTHERS

"Great companies are not always headed up by great leadership, yet great companies that last and improve are!"

ADDING TO OTHERS

"What can WE learn today?
In order to teach, we've first gotta be
willing to listen and learn."

ADDING TO OTHERS

"You'll only push other people
to do their best
if you're pushing the envelope."

ADDING TO OTHERS

PHASE 6

CONSISTENCY

"How consistent you can be with pursuing progress will ultimately be who are you in that craft."

CONSISTENCY

"Stay consistently looking to get better. Many of us go for a little while and give up, not realizing that success may be just behind the next door."

CONSISTENCY

"To become your best takes an
intense amount of focus.
And the end results are what make
the process so desirable."

CONSISTENCY

"Have a relationship with
the work and the workout and
you'll watch yourself
continue to improve, no doubt."

CONSISTENCY

"You won't become good or great in the light. Light will only show goodness and greatness that's earned in the dark."

CONSISTENCY

"If you can see the goal, keep working... If you can't see the goal, start working..."

CONSISTENCY

"If you have a job, or a craft, and a detail has to be explained to you more than twice, it COULD be the reason your opportunity is lost.
Get good at the details."

CONSISTENCY

"Getting up and getting your work in, is a choice; it's not an ability or condition you're born with."

CONSISTENCY

"Remind yourself to make it fun. That business. That sport. That relationship. Remind yourself to make it fun."

CONSISTENCY

"That work today, won't show until tomorrow. Just keep going."

CONSISTENCY

"It's challenging to become great, stay great, or remain great on your own."

CONSISTENCY

"It's disrespectful to give an opponent or competitor only 75 percent of your effort."

CONSISTENCY

"If you're not working on your game
of life every day, then you're looking to
get leap-frogged by those around you,
putting in work, consistently."

CONSISTENCY

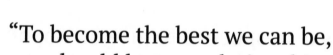

"To become the best we can be,
we should have a relationship
with the work. After a little while,
it'll no longer be work."

CONSISTENCY

"Action is the loudest voice..."

CONSISTENCY

"Consistent effort is the staple of greatness."

CONSISTENCY

Take a Deep Breath.

You have completed the first section of

BECOME YOUR BEST
Be proud of yourself.

Now you will experience Chris P Austin's commentary on each of his quotes. With that commentary, you will gain insight on how he translates the quotes, which will provoke your own thought on how you are learning it, and ultimately, how you will understand it.

> # Your Confidence
> # is worth
> # investing in.
> — CHRIS P AUSTIN

PHASE 1

AWARENESS

"If you aren't in the position you want
to be in on the
team/business/relationship,
have a transparent conversation
with the leader...
and then you become a leader."

Chris' Commentary:

Our natural instinct is to spend and
plan for the more material and more
tangible things. Mentality is the pilot
light to what creates REAL
happiness. So, invest your time,
money, and energy into that.

"Remember the power of believing in yourself."

Chris' Commentary:

Those in challenging moments, and unprecedented moments, as well as simple moments have had their greatest results and largest breakthroughs, not when they phoned a friend, not when they consulted the audience, definitely not when they took a pass... but when THEY believed.

"Going for it will give you the best
opportunity to be successful.
If you don't go for it, you, for sure,
won't be successful."

Chris' Commentary:

Many of the people I work with or
have known come into the
relationship with a fear of
confrontation or a discomfort with the
result going against what he or she
wants. Being able to create a different
reality begins with that conversation.

"The most successful people in the world are those who understand the importance of happiness... real happiness.
Happiness is success."

Chris' Commentary:

Historic stories of success always began with a trial and error. Lack of securing clients, breakups, and missed shots in basketball are the beginning of championship winning shots, your greatest relationship, and consistent clientele.

"At a high level, most have talent and ability and experience.
What separates success and happiness is mentality."

Chris' Commentary:

Starting a business or Fortune 500, 50 years happily connected with someone or the first fun date, JV tennis or Serena Williams' career... mentality is what makes the difference, far more than the physical.

"You don't have to be born a champion to become a champion."

Chris' Commentary:

More people than I can count have come to me and stated why they can or cannot do something because of some previous result they had already experienced. We always have the ability to change our reality, so decide if you want the same reality or a different one.

"The most we've ever seen someone learn, is when they were willing."

Chris' Commentary:

High achievers become obsessed with learning and improving. If you look at the career of what business person, what person in a relationship, or what sports person you admire, I would be willing to bet that there was a new achievement and a new personal record for them with each new year.

"Invite in understanding.
Understanding is the beginning
of progress.
Choosing not to TRY & understand
keeps us standing still."

Chris' Commentary:

Understanding is different from
judging. Judgement is natural.
Understanding is a skill that we must
train in order to become our best.

"The best way to make it better begins with a conversation. However, it doesn't end with a conversation. Actions speak."

Chris' Commentary:

Once you've gotten bold enough to have that conversation and talk that talk, you better put the action with it next. Words matter, yet, they get lost without some show of the advertisement.

"There are many ways to become great,
yet very few ways to make the decision."

Chris' Commentary:

I have had intro conversations time and
again where people have told me that
something is not their style or just not
the way they do things. How we choose
to do anything is a decision. Direct
and focused time and energy is how to
become great.

"Becoming great at your craft requires so much little detail in the shadows. These current shadows can be used."

Chris' Commentary:

You're reading this book because you should be reading this book. Gather all the details necessary for your breakthrough and construct your action plan. Decide to become your best, rather than make an excuse of why the timing isn't right.

"Happiness will be found when hard work and time spent meet one another. Hard work + Time spent."

Chris' Commentary:

Chillin' won't satisfy your happiness repeating itself. Chillin' leads to temporary happiness. Spending time on the craft you think about most often is where your happiness will root and repeat daily.

"Your life will be what you work for.
Dust will settle on what you were born
with, and then the work...
It's never too early or too late
to learn that."

Chris' Commentary:

Where you start in life is irrelevant at
this point. If you started with no
money or a grip of money is whatever.
If you have height or strength or are
smaller or weaker does not determine
where you end up. Learn that from my
life. You can reach your goal if you GO!

"Stacking chips is the first thing you do. In standard terms that means: SAVE FIRST. The next questions are "save what?" and "save how?"

Chris' Commentary:

You don't have to save $100,000 right now. You could save $10 this week and you'd be in a better spot than you were before. It needs to be a priority if you want to sustain your happiness.

"Don't be fooled... the fastest way to the top is STILL the stairs."

Chris' Commentary:

Shortcuts right now and jumping the gun and cheating rather than waiting and anticipating will get you having to backtrack. Choose the risky grind that will have a fun adventure along the way.

"Name someone who became great to
society's standards, or felt great to
their own standard without vision...
read it again... "

Chris' Commentary:

Go ahead and read that again.

"If you want more happiness, have a relationship with the work. Work and progress invite confidence."

Chris' Commentary:

If you don't like working then adjust what you are working on. If... scratch that... When you find the craft you crave, you'll enjoy the work.

"Happiness should come before money."

Chris' Commentary:

Avoid allowing the hazy-vision-effect of pursuing money first, because there will never be enough. Learn, understand, and pursue what makes you happy.

"Don't discount the power of setting goals. It can change your life."

Chris' Commentary:

Goal setting is scientifically proven and proven by the eye-test to be the direct bridge from where you are now to where you want to be... Goal setting and reading this book... Those two things.

"The world has so few leaders.
Look around, see if that's accurate.
Then use it as an opportunity
to step up."

Chris' Commentary:

Because the world is starving for
leaders within each craft, real
thoughtful and careful leaders, you
should go ahead and step up to study
and then lead.

"If it's what YOU want to do, then you're on the right track. Keep going."

Chris' Commentary:

Others' opinions are irrelevant as it pertains to that. Keep going.

"Mistakes are real and
important. Mistake response is real
and more important."

Chris' Commentary:

Get that never-twice mentality going;
as in, go ahead and make that mistake,
just focus on that next best action
response to it. Never twice! The only
time to use never.

"You responding with how bad you are at something is the fastest way to NOT improve.
Confidence breeds results."

Chris' Commentary:

After you make a mistake or do something that wasn't your intention or slip up, work really hard at making your next comment focused on what you're going to do next. Focus on the response, rather than the slip up.

"If you've got goals to reach...
Start today."

Chris' Commentary:

Planning to start in the future lowers the percentages of the actual application. Start the process today and your percentages go way up. Progress is all about the percentages.

"If you say you want to start, then you better go ahead and start..."

Chris' Commentary:

Let's see those actions speak. We hear all that talking! Let's see that action in motion.

"This is the right time and place to start your upward trajectory to reach as high as is possible for you."

Chris' Commentary:

You're in the process right now of realizing where you want to go. Turn where you want to go into where you're going. That right there is a decision of yours and no one else's.

"There are consequences to having confidence. Accept the consequences."

Chris' Commentary:

Consequences often come with a negative connotation. A consequence is the result of an action that you chose. Let's get those results you earned.

"Belief can be trained."

Chris' Commentary:

It doesn't matter if you have no belief right now or a strong belief. What you're training right now matters, and the consistency of that.

"Are there those out there who embrace what is difficult?"

Chris' Commentary:

If you choose to embrace what is difficult, you will literally become a legend.

"Develop your opinion based on your own experiences; today and every day."

Chris' Commentary:

Another person's experience is not yours. May sound obvious... live that concept like it's obvious. Use your own.

"Let's get a little bit better today."

Chris' Commentary:

Getting a little bit better requires a strong focus and attention to detail. Work really hard for a while in order to get a little bit better. That is the truth and reality. I cannot wait until we get to phase number four.

"Life will continue to improve. It begins between the ears."

Chris' Commentary:

The experience of your life is not determined by the changes in the environment around you. Your mentality and your perspective are what shape the experience of your life.

"Mentality over Age."

Chris' Commentary:

Worrying about age and how it factors in will take you further away from your goals, and even stop you from creating goals. Mentality is where you find what matches you and your path.

PHASE 2

CONFIDENCE
COMES FROM ME

"Confidence is what separates good from great, the belief in yourself."

Chris' Commentary:

You can train your business building, your relationship and creativity, and all of your skills in your sports; yet none of those things will be staples without the foundation of real confidence.

"Mentality is something that can be taught. And having a strong confidence and understanding of how you get yourself to that place creates happiness for your life."

Chris' Commentary:

Many believe that the type of person they are was decided from birth. That is false. You can train who you want to be.

"Shoot your shot. Worst case... you're in the same position you're in now: without."

Chris' Commentary:

If you don't go for it then you'll be the same position you're in right now anyway. Make the freakin' decision to shoot that shot.

"Don't compare yourself to others.
You will never be them, and they will
never be you."

Chris' Commentary:

It's all you and you can make this your
time to shine. You can allow these
other people to hold you back or they
can drive you forward. The sure thing
for you to go forward is to take it into
your hands. Compare yourself to
where you were yesterday and build,
every day.

"If you aren't believing in you...
all the technical and hands-on training
will be a waste.
Success begins with believing in you."

Chris' Commentary:

Invest in your confidence. That is what
will get you to a new level faster than
anything technical.

"Becoming your own biggest fan will lead you to more happiness much faster. Then you'll really be able to help others."

Chris' Commentary:

Let's be for real right now. If someone asked you right now, who your favorite person is, would you say yourself?... Why or why not?

"Taking stress away from your life begins with taking away the value of outside opinions of yourself."

Chris' Commentary:

Valuing your own opinion the most will create less stress, if you have a good opinion. Before you can have a good opinion, you have to decide that your own opinion matters most.

"Know your value is the deal.
If you don't know your value, learn it.
If you already know it... really know it...
apply it.
You are valuable."

Chris' Commentary:

Get to the point where me telling
you that doesn't mean the most.
You telling yourself that is what
really means something. I am here
to remind you.

"Be unconcerned what the world thinks. Be concerned with what makes you improve... and then what helps others around you improve."

Chris' Commentary:

The world has continuously developing trends. Think about that for a moment; how things have changed in the last X amount of years. You can develop too, but it doesn't have to be with the world's trends. You find your happiness by understanding yourself.

"Becoming your best will be decided
by you. Others' opinions slow the process.
You go ahead and choose."

Chris' Commentary:

I don't recommend that you wait
for permission from someone else
to bet on yourself and make a
move. If you want it, then let's go!

"Quit turning your neck to find
YOUR success.
The mirror is in front of you."

Chris' Commentary:

Don't look for the team or the cheering
squad to have some achievements.
Real and sustainable achievement
comes from your work in the empty
office, in the house alone, in the gym
solo. It then, it being that leadership,
replicates itself in small crowds and big
crowds and all over the world.

"Your opinion about you is primary and most important. Make it a good one."

Chris' Commentary:

Before you can have a wonderful opinion of yourself and have that be a game-changing characteristic, you must first consistently decide that your opinion is going to be the one that matters when it comes to you.

"The importance of understanding what is beautiful about you cannot be overstated."

Chris' Commentary:

When I've worked with clients, one of the first questions I ask them to answer in the beginning is, "What are two traits about yourself that you enjoy?" which is often followed with a long pause or a delayed response... and I ask, "What is one thing you'd like to improve or adjust?" which is often responded to swiftly and with more than one add-on. By the end of working with me, the responses to those questions have the opposite reaction and response speed. Understand what's beautiful about you.

"Know what's valuable about yourself... then add."

Chris' Commentary:

Be in a daily search for what makes you wonderfully different as well as what is it about you that has the potential to connect to other people.

"Your best is determined by doing all you can with what YOU have. Although others can help, your best isn't determined by other people."

Chris' Commentary:

Your instinct can tell you where you can go. Once you've found that instinctual point that you can get to, realize you can go further. The human output can always go longer than the human mind hypothesizes.

"Tell yourself... that you believe in yourself. You'll be closer."

Chris' Commentary:

It begins with your words and then stretches to your actions. It begins with words.

"Tell yourself three GOOD and very different things about yourself today. Lather. Rinse. Repeat."

Chris' Commentary:

Imagine hitting that process on repeat for one week. Start today my person.

"Learn as quickly as possible, that there is only one person who can REALLY tell you that you're good or not good."

Chris' Commentary:

See... at this point in the book you already know who that person is. Let's get it.

"If you want to be a beast, quit telling yourself you're a weenie."

Chris' Commentary:

How you speak is the start. How you speak mentally and how you speak verbally.

"You are in charge of where you get to. Enjoy that responsibility and embrace it."

Chris' Commentary:

Don't fear having a bunch on your plate or feeling like it's too much right now. You can handle it. Be cool with being in charge.

"It can be as simple as telling yourself YOU CAN DO IT."

Chris' Commentary:

For today that is really all that you need to get better. The next step will be taking action to make sure it's more than words. Right now, say it out loud. Don't be nervous and don't be ashamed. Say it.

"Greatness has a common thread:
it believes in itself the most.
It may have fans, supporters, and a
push sometimes... however, it doesn't
require that.. And it MUST believe in
itself. Any great person, place or thing."

Chris' Commentary:

Any great noun has those
characteristics. The way you do it will
be unique, but not unique by choice.
Instead, unique by nature. Fight for
that belief today, whether it's an easy
fight or a challenging fight.

"How special you are isn't determined by your parents or your kids. You be the show."

Chris' Commentary:

For your parents and your kids, 'special' is determined by them. And you don't get to be special because you were born or because you woke up today. You have to work for the status of special. Let's work.

"That which you seek, should show attraction back to you, in order for it to become a thing. Business, crafts, sports, relationships, etc..."

Chris' Commentary:

Understand the difference between a challenge with small progressions, ultimately working toward achieving a larger goal, versus pursuing a craft that clearly does not want you how you want it. Symmetry is something you can feel and you become happy with the challenging pursuit. That is your search.

"The world isn't waiting for you to be ready. Just decide you're ready."

Chris' Commentary:

If you wait, today's opportunity is going to pass by. Take advantage today. I am telling you that your best shot at making it happen is going after it right now, today.

"We are in control of how we respond...
to all things verbal, emotional,
and mental."

Chris' Commentary:

Don't say they made you do it or you
didn't want to cause a problem. If you
aren't happy then change is required.
For change to happen, you have to
address the problem with the current
state of affairs.

"Notice yourself, and you won't require someone else's attention."

Chris' Commentary:

This is a dope quote... Have you looked in the mirror lately and just smiled? Perhaps it is time for that to happen for you. Find the beauty, because it is there.

"Being great does require gaining confidence from someone. That someone would be you..."

Chris' Commentary:

Who's your greatest influence? You. Who is your biggest fan? You. Who do you go to when you need to have a challenge solved? You go to you. All because you're training for that. You are made for that.

"Yourself is what YOU CHOOSE...
it's not something you were born and
destined to be... or someone you were
raised to be... WHO YOU ARE
is a choice of yours."

Chris' Commentary:

Forget the trends and dig deep to
know what it is that makes you
happier. When you focus on being
happy, the rest comes to you. I
promise.

"Your best chance of getting seen is being the first to believe in your vision."

Chris' Commentary:

If you really want to be seen then you have to see yourself first. You don't get discovered because someone else saw you and you never saw it. Go for the dream and the visual of you will follow.

"Believe in your ability to create great."

Chris' Commentary:

Going from good to great takes confidence. You truly have the ability to create great. Each person does, actually. Why the majority of people don't create great is because they won't even start, let alone finish, the pursuit.

"If it wasn't for the struggle then you wouldn't be you."

Chris' Commentary:

I said this in my own mind and then I heard Two Chainz, the musical artist, say it in a rap... so i knew it had to be true. LOL

"Confidence is in our control."

Chris' Commentary:

This is just an important one for you to remember and be reminded of today. Replication is how a habit is built. Represent it. Replicate it.

PHASE 3

ADDING TO MYSELF

"The same person you see in your head is the same person you are. Those persons can be developed."

Chris' Commentary:

If you say that you cannot do it, you are correct. If you say that you can do it, you are correct. Make your statement, my person.

"Break down the barriers of potential and unlock the stratosphere of progress."

Chris' Commentary:

The way that you perform this Shakespearean stuff is going for it today. Tomorrow, today's opportunities will have passed. Tomorrow, the opportunities will be new.

"People want to connect with whoever or whatever is going to be their bridge... without realizing that they, themselves, are the bridge."

Chris' Commentary:

Once you have realized the reality of this concept that confidence coming from you will be the foundation of your confidence being sustained, now it's time to solidify why you will become as good as you can become, your best.

"Saving money isn't just for when you're making a relatively large amount of money. Saving a percentage is for always."

Chris' Commentary:

Feeling solid financially is a large part of overall life confidence. How you get yourself to that point is adding to your savings.

"Working out your body is a portion of becoming your best."

Chris' Commentary:

Exercise is a must in adding to the complete version of you. You don't have to be an Olympic athlete... or you can be. Exercise every week will change your life for the better.

"Being vocal or assertive or in front isn't something you're born with or a privilege at birth. It's a decision you make on a daily basis."

Chris' Commentary:

Communication is one of the three things that connects people, in addition to music, and sports. Communicate to be more connected.

"Be multifaceted and you'll have multiple opportunities."

Chris' Commentary:

If you have multiple skills, that will make you more successful. Work on your skills today.

"No matter your childhood experience, everyone can find lessons in their upbringing... and current life."

Chris' Commentary:

Memory is a dangerous tool if you have negative connotation. Memory is a powerful tool if it is utilized for how to create success.

"Competition is how to get to a new level. Competition with self is the best kind."

Chris' Commentary:

Lock in on how you can become better than you were yesterday. If you improve every day, you are going to reach your goals.

"Become great at controlling
the pace of your life.
Then the world's pace won't
matter much."

Chris' Commentary:

You can absolutely handle improving
your pace. What has to be trained is
your organization. The more organized
you are, the better your pace can be.

"Being willing to work is what gets you
to the next level.
Sitting back and waiting is rare
to get results. Go get it!"

Chris' Commentary:

Often my clients ask how they can
choose to do the things that they want
to do rather than easy things like
laying down and watching TV. The
concept that we go over is adding to
themselves.

"Working out isn't a waste of time.
It's time well spent.
Find your time and workout your body.
Workout your mind."

Chris' Commentary:

If you can get your body to sweat from a workout, it will engage the portions of your brain that are most responsible for creative thinking.

"Competing against others will give you gains. Competing against yourself will give you greater gains."

Chris' Commentary:

If you can develop a healthy relationship with yourself, you will be able to compete, and attack, and understand, and grind into a new level of execution. You cannot be scared to feel a little dip in order to have a massive rise in improvement.

"Youth & adults: look to handle your own responsibilities. More confidence comes with doing your own work."

Chris' Commentary:

Don't have mommy and daddy do it for you. Don't have your teacher or coach or mentor handle it for you. The experience that you gain from doing it yourself, as the world will show in the championship.

"The WHOLE deal is challenge-solving.
Learn to solve challenges and
you'll really enjoy your life.
Make this day what you want it to be."

Chris' Commentary:

Don't complain about the problem.
Drive towards that solution.
There will be some steps in between.
Start cranking today.

"Invite less "seeing what others can do" into your stuff. Invite more "seeing what I (you) will do"."

Chris' Commentary:

There is no feeling on earth like receiving a goal that you set, knowing that you drove the achievement of it.

"The number one way to gain experience is to travel. Outside of your house, outside of your city, outside of your state/country, outside of that COMFORT!"

Chris' Commentary:

In business, in relationships, in sports, and all things that are a craft, experience wins the majority. Experience with strong mentality wins every time. Shout out to Michael Jordan.

"The grind isn't waiting for you to have more energy. Helping yourself and others become as good as possible can give you energy."

Chris' Commentary:

If you feel tired right now, try getting into a dedicated thing that you are driven toward. Even if there is no money right now. Let's find out the energy that you have toward what you actually care about.

"If you want to get to a new level,
you'll have to be alright with
the temporary dip, before
you shoot it through the roof."

Chris' Commentary:

Before any great achievement, is a little
bit of downward movement while
learning the new process. Be OK with
that while you get on your way to
shooting it through the roof and
crushing it.

"If you feel like you're at the top... build some new floors at your building."

Chris' Commentary:

Stop playin'... You have not arrived.

"Any person can have an ideal environment. Being able to exist->succeed->thrive in ANY environment is what makes full-time value."

Chris' Commentary:

If you can get that chameleon effect going... You will reach your goals. I personally thrive in the chameleon mode, and lion mentality.

"Get in the figurative kitchen and bake
your dreams into reality."

Chris' Commentary:

Get your Top Chef on, Wolfgang Puck.

"Wake up lookin' to make a life better and more meaningful... start with your own, and then branch."

Chris' Commentary:

Being able to help another person progress, really begins with the way that you model. Human beings can sense when something they are watching is for real. Be for real, in order to help.

"If you are going to talk,
talk about what you're going to do,
rather than what you're
NOT going to do. Serves more purpose."

Chris' Commentary:

I personally don't really want to hear
about what you are not going to do.
I want to hear about what you are going
to do. Let's hear it.

"Quit doing stuff for the money and you'll be closer to the happiness you seek."

Chris' Commentary:

Pursuing money as the primary will motivate you for a short amount of time, and will have you unhappy as time goes on. Pursue happiness, and money will not be an issue.

"Tomorrow I will become greater than I was today... at life."

Chris' Commentary:

I am super hopeful that you read this as yourself, and not as 'What Chris is going to do'. Either way, now you know that the quote in the message are for you.

"Becoming a champion is at
the tips of your fingers and lips,
you just have to start."

Chris' Commentary:

What I mean by that is that you have to
begin saying it, that it is possible. After
that, you begin doing it, and if you
keep doing it, it will be possible.

"Each (fill in) can be great.
We have to make it reality.
Like anything worth having."

Chris' Commentary:

Anything worth having, anything
worth doing, anything worth spending
time on, anything worth it...

"Get in some gratitude before
you get your day going.
However things are, they could be worse.
And however things are,
you can make them even better."

Chris' Commentary:

The point of this is that it does not
really matter how things are. It matters
what you are going to choose to do.

"End up where you are on purpose.
Don't let it be an accident."

Chris' Commentary:

And then after you do it, let's see you
do it again to make sure that it was not
an accident.

PHASE 4

URGENCY
IDEOLOGY

"The time is now.
Waiting is a waste of time."

Chris' Commentary:

I hope that you put this book aside (for now), and go straight to making it happen. Go ahead. Right now. This book will be here waiting for your return.

"Later is not the best time to get it done. Now..."

Chris' Commentary:

I want to point out that this concept is a habit, from things like taking out the trash, to writing that book you want to publish, to becoming a CEO. Now is how.

"The time to jump on the train isn't later... the train is leaving."

Chris' Commentary:

Reading this book helps you punch your ticket. No more money necessary in order to get on the train.

"Waiting for the right time is allowing the right time to pass you by. The right time is right now."

Chris' Commentary:

In the past, taking immediate action may have been challenging. Now, you have plenty of reasons to go for it. And not just once. Again and again. Waiting adds more anxiety, more fear, more hesitation. Jump in the pool. Take the dive. Go for it.

"The want won't ever be stronger than the need. Pursue what you need in order to be successful. I'm on that tip."

Chris' Commentary:

I would like for you to get on that tip with me. Keep reading, we will learn exactly what I mean.

"Trying your hardest IS enough... if it's really your hardest."

Chris' Commentary:

Where most get caught up in terms of this concept, is that they say that they are trying their hardest, however, it is not really their hardest. It must be your hardest.

"Having the discipline to receive
and NOT spend right away
is the start of feeling solid financially.
Receive and assess."

Chris' Commentary:

If you really want the money situation
to be on point, start saving. The new
Bentley, figuratively or literally, can
wait. And, if you aren't going to really
value it, don't buy it.

"Go ahead and reach for the top of the mountain... realize you aren't there... keep going."

Chris' Commentary:

This epitomizes urgency ideology. Pursue perfection, and then be understanding that perfection won't come. Appreciate the progress you made.

"Because the world is different doesn't mean you can't still get to your goals. This is where those who practice mental toughness rise up."

Chris' Commentary:

The people who ultimately change the world, whether it is a scientist creating a vaccine, an athlete breaking a record, or a lawyer advancing human rights... Once upon a time their vision was the minority, not the majority.

"If you don't do it, there is less of a guarantee that it gets done.
So Nike... just do it."

Chris' Commentary:

You really do not have to wait. Shout out to Nike for this one.

"Go for it today. You won't get this day back."

Chris' Commentary:

It is super important that we realize that days are not unlimited. Because of that, it is important that you make the most of today. Get closer to the goals you want to reach. Don't blame it on doing research, or waiting for the right time. Now is the right time.

"Tomorrow isn't the day to work
at what you want.
Today is the day to go get it."

Chris' Commentary:

Yesterday isn't the day either to worry
about what you did. Today is the day.
Let's go.

"Challenge your limits, and take chances.
The alternative is having no chance..."

Chris' Commentary:

Be bold, or perish... LOL

"It's unlikely you'll maximize your
potential by hedging your bets.
If you wait to get out of your first thing,
while you get your next thing setup...
someone is likely passing you up.
Just go now!"

Chris' Commentary:

Drop whatever you are doing now that
is not working toward your ultimate goal.
Even if it's scary, go toward your goal.

"To have great influence requires
great sacrifice.
So decide to enjoy that challenge."

Chris' Commentary:

On the micro scale, and macro scale of
influence, this concept is important to
understand. Sacrifice the things that
don't matter as much as your goal.

"Avoid being satisfied with the result.
Look for that satisfaction after the work.
Then you're going somewhere."

Chris' Commentary:

If you can train your satisfaction to be
with dedication and focus during the
work, rather than the potential to gain
an award, you will rise to the level of
the top performers in the world.

"If this life were your only chance...
what would your goals be?"

Chris' Commentary:

How enormous would your goals be?
How outrageous would your vision be?
Now, just do that.

"Treat the week like it's your only one.
Go after what you want now!
Next week is too late."

Chris' Commentary:

If you had one week to pursue everything you wanted, what would you do? If you would go into hyperfocus, then, do that now. You won't regret it.

"It's not always going to be perfect."

Chris' Commentary:

But I would prefer that you pursue that perfection, yet to realize and avoid frustration with the thought that perfection won't come.

"If today were the first... If today were the last... What would you do?"

Chris' Commentary:

The real answer that I would ask myself in the situation, is if those two answers are the same. If they are not the same, then I've got to spend time on making them the same. If they were the same, that would be a sign that I am living my best life.

PHASE 5

ADDING TO OTHERS

"Creating opportunities for others
will create opportunities for yourself."

Chris' Commentary:

If you can truly go into your craft now
trying to build for others, without
losing sight of yourself, you personally
will absolutely build in opportunities
and happiness.

"A starting point is surrounding yourself
with those who desire
upward and forward movement.
Success CAN begin alone...
it only grows with community, though."

Chris' Commentary:

Now you are ready to learn phase 5.
Take an inventory of your community.

"Show them you care about their progress as much as they do."

Chris' Commentary:

This is the real start to building a great team around you in business, in a relationship, and in sports. Make it a priority. With a great team, you can influence more.

"What creates is our ability to raise the level of ourselves and others. What tears down is trying to shove down others for our gain."

Chris' Commentary:

Don't make the mistake of believing that someone else has to drop down for you to rise up. If others rise, and you are competitive, you will feel it subconsciously, and if you are competing with yourself, as you should be, you will do some of your best work.

"Good leaders don't pick a side to
support. The best leaders help
all parties understand."

Chris' Commentary:

This applies in business, and politics,
and relationships, and athletics, the
entire world. Great leaders have a way
of bringing people together for
communication. That "way" is
practiced and trained.

"Step One: make yourself as good as you can today. Step Two: help others get as good as they can. The best way to help another is to show the demo... do it yourself."

Chris' Commentary:

Be the demonstration of what a real boost in confidence is, and how that can affect achievement. Make sure the boost of confidence is something we see from you every day.

"You don't have to deal with anyone
who you feel is acting wild.
Yet, you should make an effort to create
community."

Chris' Commentary:

You can walk away. If it is a safe
environment the next level would be
working hard to create understanding
with that person.

"How much better can you make
yourself this week?
Realizing others will watch,
and follow suit."

Chris' Commentary:

The thread of commonality that you
are noticing is that why you
maximizing and showing your best,
lifts the others around you to do the
same.

"Make someone else smile today.
Stuff is contagious."

Chris' Commentary:

Tell the truth, do you feel good when
you smile? Imagine if you could create
that for someone else, by just you
doing it. Reality check... You can.
Curve those corners up.

"Keep the hard workers around you, then embrace the competition."

Chris' Commentary:

The best team is not full of people who say yes. The best team respectfully challenges, and creates thoughtful conversation. The thoughtful conversation should lead to actionable takeaways.

"The most productive way to help others is by showing how, rather than doing for."

Chris' Commentary:

If you bring a woman or man a fish, she or he will be fed for the meal. If you teach a man or woman to fish, he or she will be fed for a lifetime.

"The majority of what you tell people you're critiquing should not be what they are doing wrong.
Teach how. Teach confidence."

Chris' Commentary:

The concept that I do not see used frequently enough in coaching, is simply telling a person what to do rather than, or in addition to, what not to do.

"Motivate into momentum."

Chris' Commentary:

That is what I am doing for you. Helping you realize what you already have, so that you can take action. Once you've taken action, you begin to add things that you do not already have. Once you have added those, you can add to others.

"Great companies are not always headed up by great leadership, yet great companies that last and improve are!"

Chris' Commentary:

Great leadership does not have to be the picture of what you have seen in the movies. Great leadership has the traits learned in these 6 Phases.

"What can WE learn today?
In order to teach, we've first gotta be
willing to listen and learn."

Chris' Commentary:

This is a check-in quote for you. Great
teachers are great at learning. If you
really want to become your best,
become a serial and lifelong learner.

"You'll only push other people
to do their best
if you're pushing the envelope."

Chris' Commentary:

As humans, we can inherently feel if
someone or something is giving their
best. Although other people's opinions
don't matter, your opinion does, so
make it obvious that you are giving
everything you have to the progress and
ultimate goal of becoming your best.

PHASE 6

CONSISTENCY

"How consistent you can be with pursuing progress will ultimately be who are you in that craft."

Chris' Commentary:

You don't want to be a one-hit wonder in your craft. For you to become your best, requires you diving into this consistently.

"Stay consistently looking to get better. Many of us go for a little while and give up, not realizing that success may be just behind the next door."

Chris' Commentary:

But don't even try peeking behind the door, AKA trying to fortune-tell the future. Don't even look for the trophy. Enjoy the process and the work.

"To become your best takes an
intense amount of focus.
And the end results are what make
the process so desirable."

Chris' Commentary:

You have made it this far through this
book, and clearly you want to get to
this goal of becoming your best. Begin
the serious focus on your consistency.

"Have a relationship with
the work and the workout and
you'll watch yourself
continue to improve, no doubt."

Chris' Commentary:

During this process, the importance of
physical energy being utilized and
pushed should not be lost. Mentality is
primary; verbal energy is important.
Preparing your body physically is also
necessary to sustain your effort.

"You won't become good or great in the light. Light will only show goodness and greatness that's earned in the dark."

Chris' Commentary:

Beyond your business meetings and clocked hours, beyond your fun weekends away and family gatherings, further than your team practices and the games themselves, there must be a relationship to the work when no one is watching.

"If you can see the goal, keep working...
If you can't see the goal, start working..."

Chris' Commentary:

If you are not working yet at this stuff
every single day, you have not been
paying attention. Pay attention. Focus.

"If you have a job, or a craft, and a detail has to be explained to you more than twice, it COULD be the reason your opportunity is lost.
Get good at the details."

Chris' Commentary:

Being able to hear it, see it, watch it, feel it is ultimately how you will reach this goal of becoming your best.

"Getting up and getting your work in,
is a choice; it's not an ability or condition
you're born with."

Chris' Commentary:

There are zero people stopping you.
Make that decision. You are the only
person who would even have the
opportunity to stop you, and there's
no way you are going to do that.

"Remind yourself to make it fun. That business. That sport. That relationship. Remind yourself to make it fun."

Chris' Commentary:

The grind can get challenging. Remind yourself about why you started.
How much you enjoy the craft is why you started.

"That work today, won't show until tomorrow. Just keep going."

Chris' Commentary:

Just know that in the back of your mind. And don't even look forward to seeing the show. Make the most of this process.

"It's challenging to become great, stay great, or remain great on your own."

Chris' Commentary:

Is this a challenge you are willing to accept? I know you are. You are reading this book.

"It's disrespectful to give an opponent
or competitor only 75 percent of your
effort."

Chris' Commentary:

Now that you have arrived upon this
competitive version of yourself, don't
be too cool, too busy, too tired to give
everything you got.

"If you're not working on your game of life every day, then you're looking to get leap-frogged by those around you, putting in work, consistently."

Chris' Commentary:

You are understanding the 6 Phase process. Don't stop. And don't look in your rearview mirror. Get to a new level.

"To become the best we can be,
we should have a relationship
with the work. After a little while,
it'll no longer be work."

Chris' Commentary:

It will be all you know. You will have
what you want.

"Action is the loudest voice..."

Chris' Commentary:

You are going to require this concept
every day from here on out.

"Consistent effort is the staple of greatness."

Chris' Commentary:

You are loved.

Chris P Austin developed the 6 Phase process by compiling all of his coaching experiences and creating a system that can be used by any human.

Chris P Austin coaching families.

Chris P Austin coaching business.

Chris P Austin coaching youth mentality.

Chris P Austin during a retreat.

The moment Chris P Austin realized that championships come from mentality far more than they do talent.

Chris P Austin with his first book
"The Way: A Hawaiian Story Of Growth, Relationships, & Volleyball".

Chris P Austin with his mother, doing her favorite thing... shopping.

You have just completed the second section of

BECOME YOUR BEST

During this process of reading the quotes, feeling how they should be applied and transformed into action is the gift. Subconsciously you are learning to understand my 6 Phase process to mastering confidence.

Mastering confidence will be the key to the lock of your maximum productivity and achievement.

In Section 3, I would like for you to have a pen, as well as a pencil. The pen is for you to write down your very first interpretation of the quote as you read it in Section 3. The pencil is for you to have the opportunity to record, as well as erase and re-record your thoughts, feelings, interpretation, and most importantly, how you'd like to remember the quote.

> # Your Confidence
> ## is worth
> ## investing in.
> —— CHRIS P AUSTIN ——

PHASE 1

AWARENESS

"If you aren't in the position you want to be in on the team/business/relationship, have a transparent conversation with the leader... and then you become a leader."

In Pen:

If you are not Where you want
to be or not satisfied with your role
on a team, talk to the leader to find
out What you can do to achieve greatness
or the version of yourself you want to be.

In Pencil:

"Remember the power of believing in yourself."

In Pen:

Believing in yourself goes a long way

In Pencil:

"Going for it will give you the best opportunity to be successful.
If you don't go for it, you, for sure, won't be successful."

In Pen:

If you dont go for it, you will never become who you want to be. You will be disappointed by the outcome if you dont give it your all.

In Pencil:

"The most successful people in the world are those who understand the importance of happiness... real happiness.
Happiness is success."

In Pen:

If you aren't happy with what you are doing, you wont want to put in the extra step to become great.

In Pencil:

"At a high level, most have talent and ability and experience.
What separates success and happiness is mentality."

In Pen:

People can get really good at what they
are doing, but if they dont have the
happiness, it is different than success.

In Pencil:

"You don't have to be born a champion to become a champion."

In Pen:

You are not born great. You have to put in the work to become a champion. Anyone can put in the work to achieve greatness.

In Pencil:

"The most we've ever seen someone learn, is when they were willing."

In Pen:

You have to be willing to put in the work to achieve your potential.

In Pencil:

"Invite in understanding. Understanding is the beginning of progress. Choosing not to TRY & understand keeps us standing still."

In Pen:

Understanding why you are doing
something is the first step to reaching
a goal.

In Pencil:

"The best way to make it better begins with a conversation. However, it doesn't end with a conversation. Actions speak."

In Pen:

If you want to be better, then you need to talk about wanting to be better. Then you need to put in the work to do so.

In Pencil:

"There are many ways to become great, yet very few ways to make the decision."

In Pen:

There are many different paths to become what you want to be, but you have to commit to the process.

In Pencil:

"Becoming great at your craft requires so much little detail in the shadows. These current shadows can be used."

In Pen:

If you want to become great, you
have to focus on details, even if those
details are small and hard to see.

In Pencil:

"Happiness will be found when hard work and time spent meet one another. Hard work + Time spent."

In Pen:

You will be happy with yourself
when hard work is done. You will feel
like you accomplished something.

In Pencil:

"Your life will be what you work for. Dust will settle on what you were born with, and then the work... It's never too early or too late to learn that."

In Pen:

Even if you start with alot, the person who works harder, or from the bottom will come out on top.

In Pencil:

"Stacking chips is the first thing you do. In standard terms that means: SAVE FIRST. The next questions are "save what?" and "save how?"

In Pen:

Save everything you have such as skills, they will be useful later.

In Pencil:

"Don't be fooled... the fastest way to the top is STILL the stairs."

In Pen:

You can't go in a straight line to the top, you have to improve bit by bit.

In Pencil:

"Name someone who became great to society's standards, or felt great to their own standard without vision... read it again... "

In Pen:

Someone didn't get to the top without a drive or way to get there

In Pencil:

"If you want more happiness, have a relationship with the work. Work and progress invite confidence."

In Pen:

In Pencil:

"Happiness should come before money."

In Pen:

_____

_____

_____

_____

In Pencil:

_____

_____

_____

_____

"Don't discount the power of setting goals. It can change your life."

In Pen:

_____

_____

_____

_____

_____

In Pencil:

_____

_____

_____

_____

_____

"The world has so few leaders.
Look around, see if that's accurate.
Then use it as an opportunity
to step up."

In Pen:

_____

_____

_____

_____

_____

In Pencil:

_____

_____

_____

_____

_____

"If it's what YOU want to do, then you're on the right track. Keep going."

In Pen:

_____

_____

_____

_____

_____

In Pencil:

_____

_____

_____

_____

_____

"Mistakes are real and important. Mistake response is real and more important."

In Pen:

_____

_____

_____

_____

_____

In Pencil:

_____

_____

_____

_____

_____

"You responding with how bad you are at something is the fastest way to NOT improve.
Confidence breeds results."

In Pen:

_____

_____

_____

_____

_____

In Pencil:

_____

_____

_____

_____

_____

"If you've got goals to reach...
Start today."

In Pen:

_____

_____

_____

_____

_____

In Pencil:

_____

_____

_____

_____

_____

"If you say you want to start, then you better go ahead and start..."

In Pen:

In Pencil:

"This is the right time and place to start your upward trajectory to reach as high as is possible for you."

In Pen:

_____

_____

_____

_____

_____

In Pencil:

_____

_____

_____

_____

_____

"There are consequences to having confidence. Accept the consequences."

In Pen:

_____

_____

_____

_____

In Pencil:

_____

_____

_____

_____

"Belief can be trained."

In Pen:

_____

_____

_____

_____

In Pencil:

_____

_____

_____

_____

"Are there those out there who embrace what is difficult?"

In Pen:

_____

_____

_____

_____

In Pencil:

_____

_____

_____

_____

"Develop your opinion based on your own experiences; today and every day."

In Pen:

_____

_____

_____

_____

In Pencil:

_____

_____

_____

_____

"Let's get a little bit better today."

In Pen:

_____

_____

_____

_____

_____

In Pencil:

_____

_____

_____

_____

_____

"Life will continue to improve.
It begins between the ears."

In Pen:

_____

_____

_____

_____

_____

In Pencil:

_____

_____

_____

_____

_____

"Mentality over age."

In Pen:

_____

_____

_____

_____

_____

In Pencil:

_____

_____

_____

_____

_____

PHASE 2

CONFIDENCE
COMES FROM ME

"Confidence is what separates good from great, the belief in yourself."

In Pen:

_____

_____

_____

_____

In Pencil:

_____

_____

_____

_____

"Mentality is something that can be taught. And having a strong confidence and understanding of how you get yourself to that place creates happiness for your life."

In Pen:

_____

_____

_____

_____

In Pencil:

_____

_____

_____

_____

"Shoot your shot. Worst case... you're in the same position you're in now: without."

In Pen:

_____

_____

_____

_____

In Pencil:

_____

_____

_____

_____

"Don't compare yourself to others. You will never be them, and they will never be you."

In Pen:

_____

_____

_____

_____

In Pencil:

_____

_____

_____

_____

"If you aren't believing in you... all the technical and hands-on training will be a waste. Success begins with believing in you."

In Pen:

_____

_____

_____

_____

_____

In Pencil:

_____

_____

_____

_____

_____

"Becoming your own biggest fan will lead you to more happiness much faster. Then you'll really be able to help others."

In Pen:

_____

_____

_____

_____

In Pencil:

_____

_____

_____

_____

"Taking stress away from your life begins with taking away the value of outside opinions of yourself."

In Pen:

_____

_____

_____

_____

_____

In Pencil:

_____

_____

_____

_____

_____

"Know your value is the deal.
If you don't know your value, learn it.
If you already know it... really know it...
apply it.
You are valuable."

In Pen:

_____

_____

_____

_____

In Pencil:

_____

_____

_____

_____

"Be unconcerned what the world thinks. Be concerned with what makes you improve... and then what helps others around you improve."

In Pen:

_____

_____

_____

_____

In Pencil:

_____

_____

_____

_____

"Becoming your best will be decided by you. Others' opinions slow the process. You go ahead and choose."

In Pen:

_____

_____

_____

_____

_____

In Pencil:

_____

_____

_____

_____

_____

"Quit turning your neck to find YOUR success.
The mirror is in front of you."

In Pen:

_____

_____

_____

_____

In Pencil:

_____

_____

_____

_____

"Your opinion about you is primary and most important. Make it a good one."

In Pen:

_____

_____

_____

_____

In Pencil:

_____

_____

_____

_____

"The importance of understanding what is beautiful about you cannot be overstated."

In Pen:

_____

_____

_____

_____

In Pencil:

_____

_____

_____

_____

"Know what's valuable about yourself... then add."

In Pen:

_____

_____

_____

_____

In Pencil:

_____

_____

_____

_____

"Your best is determined by doing all you can with what YOU have. Although others can help, your best isn't determined by other people."

In Pen:

_____

_____

_____

_____

In Pencil:

_____

_____

_____

_____

"Tell yourself...
that you believe in yourself.
You'll be closer."

In Pen:

_____

_____

_____

_____

In Pencil:

_____

_____

_____

_____

"Tell yourself three GOOD and very different things about yourself today. Lather. Rinse. Repeat."

In Pen:

_____

_____

_____

_____

In Pencil:

_____

_____

_____

_____

"Learn as quickly as possible, that there is only one person who can REALLY tell you that you're good or not good."

In Pen:

_____

_____

_____

_____

In Pencil:

_____

_____

_____

_____

"If you want to be a beast, quit telling yourself you're a weenie."

In Pen:

_____

_____

_____

_____

_____

In Pencil:

_____

_____

_____

_____

_____

"You are in charge of where you get to. Enjoy that responsibility and embrace it."

In Pen:

_____

_____

_____

_____

_____

In Pencil:

_____

_____

_____

_____

_____

"It can be as simple as telling yourself YOU CAN DO IT."

In Pen:

_____

_____

_____

_____

_____

In Pencil:

_____

_____

_____

_____

_____

"Greatness has a common thread:
it believes in itself the most.
It may have fans, supporters, and a
push sometimes... however, it doesn't
require that.. And it MUST believe in
itself. Any great person, place or thing."

In Pen:

_____

_____

_____

_____

_____

In Pencil:

_____

_____

_____

_____

_____

"How special you are isn't determined by your parents or your kids. You be the show."

In Pen:

_____

_____

_____

_____

In Pencil:

_____

_____

_____

_____

"That which you seek, should show attraction back to you, in order for it to become a thing. Business, crafts, sports, relationships, etc..."

In Pen:

_____

_____

_____

_____

In Pencil:

_____

_____

_____

_____

"The world isn't waiting for you to be ready. Just decide you're ready."

In Pen:

_____

_____

_____

_____

In Pencil:

_____

_____

_____

_____

"We are in control of how we respond... to all things verbal, emotional, and mental."

In Pen:

_____

_____

_____

_____

In Pencil:

_____

_____

_____

_____

"Notice yourself, and you won't require someone else's attention."

In Pen:

_____

_____

_____

_____

In Pencil:

_____

_____

_____

_____

"Being great does require gaining confidence from someone. That someone would be you..."

In Pen:

_____

_____

_____

_____

In Pencil:

_____

_____

_____

_____

"Yourself is what YOU CHOOSE...
it's not something you were born and
destined to be... or someone you were
raised to be... WHO YOU ARE
is a choice of yours."

In Pen:

_____

_____

_____

_____

_____

In Pencil:

_____

_____

_____

_____

_____

"Your best chance of getting seen is being the first to believe in your vision."

In Pen:

_____

_____

_____

_____

In Pencil:

_____

_____

_____

_____

"Believe in your ability to create great."

In Pen:

_____

_____

_____

_____

_____

In Pencil:

_____

_____

_____

_____

_____

"If it wasn't for the struggle then you wouldn't be you."

In Pen:

_____

_____

_____

_____

_____

In Pencil:

_____

_____

_____

_____

_____

"Confidence is in our control."

In Pen:

_____

_____

_____

_____

In Pencil:

_____

_____

_____

_____

PHASE 3

ADDING TO MYSELF

"The same person you see in your head is the same person you are. Those persons can be developed."

In Pen:

_____

_____

_____

_____

In Pencil:

_____

_____

_____

_____

"Break down the barriers of potential and unlock the stratosphere of progress."

In Pen:

_____

_____

_____

_____

In Pencil:

_____

_____

_____

_____

"People want to connect with whoever or whatever is going to be their bridge... without realizing that they, themselves, are the bridge."

In Pen:

_____

_____

_____

_____

In Pencil:

_____

_____

_____

_____

"Saving money isn't just for when you're making a relatively large amount of money. Saving a percentage is for always."

In Pen:

_____

_____

_____

_____

In Pencil:

_____

_____

_____

_____

"Working out your body is a portion of becoming your best."

In Pen:

_____

_____

_____

_____

_____

In Pencil:

_____

_____

_____

_____

_____

"Being vocal or assertive or in front isn't something you're born with or a privilege at birth. It's a decision you make on a daily basis."

In Pen:

_____

_____

_____

_____

_____

In Pencil:

_____

_____

_____

_____

_____

"Be multifaceted and you'll have multiple opportunities."

In Pen:

_____

_____

_____

_____

In Pencil:

_____

_____

_____

_____

"No matter your childhood experience, everyone can find lessons in their upbringing... and current life."

In Pen:

_____

_____

_____

_____

_____

In Pencil:

_____

_____

_____

_____

_____

"Competition is how to get to a new level. Competition with self is the best kind."

In Pen:

_____

_____

_____

_____

In Pencil:

_____

_____

_____

_____

"Become great at controlling the pace of your life.
Then the world's pace won't matter much."

In Pen:

_____

_____

_____

_____

In Pencil:

_____

_____

_____

_____

"Being willing to work is what gets you
to the next level.
Sitting back and waiting is rare
to get results. Go get it!"

In Pen:

_____

_____

_____

_____

_____

In Pencil:

_____

_____

_____

_____

_____

"Working out isn't a waste of time.
It's time well spent.
Find your time and workout your body.
Workout your mind."

In Pen:

_____

_____

_____

_____

In Pencil:

_____

_____

_____

_____

"Competing against others will give you gains. Competing against yourself will give you greater gains."

In Pen:

_____

_____

_____

_____

In Pencil:

_____

_____

_____

_____

"Youth & adults: look to handle your own responsibilities. More confidence comes with doing your own work."

In Pen:

_____

_____

_____

_____

In Pencil:

_____

_____

_____

_____

"The WHOLE deal is challenge-solving. Learn to solve challenges and you'll really enjoy your life. Make this day what you want it to be."

In Pen:

_____

_____

_____

_____

_____

In Pencil:

_____

_____

_____

_____

_____

"Invite less "seeing what others can do"
into your stuff. Invite more "seeing
what I (you) will do"."

In Pen:

_____

_____

_____

_____

In Pencil:

_____

_____

_____

_____

"The number one way to gain experience is to travel. Outside of your house, outside of your city, outside of your state/country, outside of that COMFORT!"

In Pen:

_____

_____

_____

_____

In Pencil:

_____

_____

_____

_____

"The grind isn't waiting for you to have more energy. Helping yourself and others become as good as possible can give you energy."

In Pen:

_____

_____

_____

_____

_____

In Pencil:

_____

_____

_____

_____

_____

"If you want to get to a new level, you'll have to be alright with the temporary dip, before you shoot it through the roof."

In Pen:

_____

_____

_____

_____

In Pencil:

_____

_____

_____

_____

"If you feel like you're at the top... build some new floors at your building."

In Pen:

_____

_____

_____

_____

_____

In Pencil:

_____

_____

_____

_____

_____

"Any person can have an ideal environment. Being able to exist->succeed->thrive in ANY environment is what makes full-time value."

In Pen:

_____

_____

_____

_____

In Pencil:

_____

_____

_____

_____

"Get in the figurative kitchen and bake your dreams into reality."

In Pen:

_____

_____

_____

_____

_____

In Pencil:

_____

_____

_____

_____

_____

"Wake up lookin' to make a life better and more meaningful... start with your own, and then branch."

In Pen:

_____

_____

_____

_____

In Pencil:

_____

_____

_____

_____

"If you are going to talk, talk about what you're going to do, rather than what you're NOT going to do. Serves more purpose."

In Pen:

_____

_____

_____

_____

In Pencil:

_____

_____

_____

_____

"Quit doing stuff for the money and you'll be closer to the happiness you seek."

In Pen:

_____

_____

_____

_____

_____

In Pencil:

_____

_____

_____

_____

_____

"Tomorrow I will become greater than I was today... at life."

In Pen:

In Pencil:

"Becoming a champion is at the tips of your fingers and lips, you just have to start."

In Pen:

_____

_____

_____

_____

In Pencil:

_____

_____

_____

_____

"Each (fill in) can be great.
We have to make it reality.
Like anything worth having."

In Pen:

_____

_____

_____

_____

_____

In Pencil:

_____

_____

_____

_____

_____

"Get in some gratitude before
you get your day going.
However things are, they could be worse.
And however things are,
you can make them even better."

In Pen:

_____

_____

_____

_____

In Pencil:

_____

_____

_____

_____

"End up where you are on purpose. Don't let it be an accident."

In Pen:

_____

_____

_____

_____

_____

In Pencil:

_____

_____

_____

_____

_____

PHASE 4

URGENCY
IDEOLOGY

"The time is now.
Waiting is a waste of time."

In Pen:

_____

_____

_____

_____

_____

In Pencil:

_____

_____

_____

_____

"Later is not the best time
to get it done. Now..."

In Pen:

_____

_____

_____

_____

In Pencil:

_____

_____

_____

_____

"The time to jump on the train isn't later... the train is leaving."

In Pen:

_____

_____

_____

_____

In Pencil:

_____

_____

_____

_____

"Waiting for the right time is allowing the right time to pass you by. The right time is right now."

In Pen:

_____

_____

_____

_____

In Pencil:

_____

_____

_____

_____

"The want won't ever be stronger than the need. Pursue what you need in order to be successful. I'm on that tip."

In Pen:

_____

_____

_____

_____

In Pencil:

_____

_____

_____

_____

"Trying your hardest IS enough... if it's really your hardest."

In Pen:

_____

_____

_____

_____

In Pencil:

_____

_____

_____

_____

"Having the discipline to receive and NOT spend right away is the start of feeling solid financially. Receive and assess."

In Pen:

_____

_____

_____

_____

In Pencil:

_____

_____

_____

_____

"Go ahead and reach for the top of the mountain... realize you aren't there... keep going."

In Pen:

_____

_____

_____

_____

_____

In Pencil:

_____

_____

_____

_____

_____

"Because the world is different doesn't mean you can't still get to your goals. This is where those who practice mental toughness rise up."

In Pen:

_____

_____

_____

_____

In Pencil:

_____

_____

_____

_____

"If you don't do it, there is less of a guarantee that it gets done. So Nike... just do it."

In Pen:

_____

_____

_____

_____

In Pencil:

_____

_____

_____

_____

"Go for it today.
You won't get this day back."

In Pen:

_____

_____

_____

_____

_____

In Pencil:

_____

_____

_____

_____

_____

"Tomorrow isn't the day to work at what you want.
Today is the day to go get it."

In Pen:

_____

_____

_____

_____

In Pencil:

_____

_____

_____

_____

"Challenge your limits, and take chances. The alternative is having no chance..."

In Pen:

_____

_____

_____

_____

In Pencil:

_____

_____

_____

_____

"It's unlikely you'll maximize your
potential by hedging your bets.
If you wait to get out of your first thing,
while you get your next thing setup...
someone is likely passing you up.
Just go now!"

In Pen:

_____

_____

_____

_____

_____

In Pencil:

_____

_____

_____

_____

_____

"To have great influence requires great sacrifice.
So decide to enjoy that challenge."

In Pen:

_____

_____

_____

_____

_____

In Pencil:

_____

_____

_____

_____

_____

"Avoid being satisfied with the result. Look for that satisfaction after the work. Then you're going somewhere."

In Pen:

_____

_____

_____

_____

_____

In Pencil:

_____

_____

_____

_____

_____

"If this life were your only chance... what would your goals be?"

In Pen:

_____

_____

_____

_____

In Pencil:

_____

_____

_____

_____

"Treat the week like it's your only one. Go after what you want now! Next week is too late."

In Pen:

_____

_____

_____

_____

_____

In Pencil:

_____

_____

_____

_____

_____

"It's not always going to be perfect."

In Pen:

_____

_____

_____

_____

In Pencil:

_____

_____

_____

_____

"If today were the first... If today were the last... What would you do?"

In Pen:

_____

_____

_____

_____

_____

In Pencil:

_____

_____

_____

_____

_____

PHASE 5

ADDING TO OTHERS

"Creating opportunities for others will create opportunities for yourself."

In Pen:

_____

_____

_____

_____

_____

In Pencil:

_____

_____

_____

_____

_____

"A starting point is surrounding yourself
with those who desire
upward and forward movement.
Success CAN begin alone...
it only grows with community, though."

In Pen:

_____

_____

_____

_____

In Pencil:

_____

_____

_____

_____

"Show them you care about their progress as much as they do."

In Pen:

_____

_____

_____

_____

_____

In Pencil:

_____

_____

_____

_____

_____

"What creates is our ability to raise the level of ourselves and others. What tears down is trying to shove down others for our gain."

In Pen:

In Pencil:

"Good leaders don't pick a side to support. The best leaders help all parties understand."

In Pen:

_____

_____

_____

_____

In Pencil:

_____

_____

_____

_____

"Step One: make yourself as good as you can today. Step Two: help others get as good as they can. The best way to help another is to show the demo... do it yourself."

In Pen:

_____

_____

_____

_____

In Pencil:

_____

_____

_____

_____

"You don't have to deal with anyone who you feel is acting wild.
Yet, you should make an effort to create community."

In Pen:

_____

_____

_____

_____

In Pencil:

_____

_____

_____

_____

"How much better can you make yourself this week? Realizing others will watch, and follow suit."

In Pen:

_____

_____

_____

_____

_____

In Pencil:

_____

_____

_____

_____

_____

"Make someone else smile today. Stuff is contagious."

In Pen:

_____

_____

_____

_____

In Pencil:

_____

_____

_____

_____

"Keep the hard workers around you, then embrace the competition."

In Pen:

_____

_____

_____

_____

In Pencil:

_____

_____

_____

_____

"The most productive way to help others is by showing how, rather than doing for."

In Pen:

_____

_____

_____

_____

_____

In Pencil:

_____

_____

_____

_____

_____

"The majority of what you tell people you're critiquing should not be what they are doing wrong.
Teach how. Teach confidence."

In Pen:

_____

_____

_____

_____

In Pencil:

_____

_____

_____

_____

"Motivate into momentum."

In Pen:

_____

_____

_____

_____

In Pencil:

_____

_____

_____

_____

"Great companies are not always headed up by great leadership, yet great companies that last and improve are!"

In Pen:

_____

_____

_____

_____

In Pencil:

_____

_____

_____

_____

"What can WE learn today?
In order to teach, we've first gotta be
willing to listen and learn."

In Pen:

_____

_____

_____

_____

In Pencil:

_____

_____

_____

_____

"You'll only push other people to do their best if you're pushing the envelope."

In Pen:

_____

_____

_____

_____

In Pencil:

_____

_____

_____

_____

PHASE 6

CONSISTENCY

"How consistent you can be with pursuing progress will ultimately be who are you in that craft."

In Pen:

_____

_____

_____

_____

In Pencil:

_____

_____

_____

_____

"Stay consistently looking to get better.
Many of us go for a little while and
give up, not realizing that success may
be just behind the next door."

In Pen:

_____

_____

_____

_____

In Pencil:

_____

_____

_____

_____

"To become your best takes an intense amount of focus. And the end results are what make the process so desirable."

In Pen:

_____

_____

_____

_____

_____

In Pencil:

_____

_____

_____

_____

_____

"Have a relationship with the work and the workout and you'll watch yourself continue to improve, no doubt."

In Pen:

_____

_____

_____

_____

In Pencil:

_____

_____

_____

_____

"You won't become good or great in the light. Light will only show goodness and greatness that's earned in the dark."

In Pen:

_____

_____

_____

_____

In Pencil:

_____

_____

_____

_____

"If you can see the goal, keep working...
If you can't see the goal, start working..."

In Pen:

_____

_____

_____

_____

_____

In Pencil:

_____

_____

_____

_____

_____

"If you have a job, or a craft, and a detail has to be explained to you more than twice, it COULD be the reason your opportunity is lost.
Get good at the details."

In Pen:

_____

_____

_____

_____

_____

In Pencil:

_____

_____

_____

_____

_____

"Getting up and getting your work in, is a choice; it's not an ability or condition you're born with."

In Pen:

_____

_____

_____

_____

_____

In Pencil:

_____

_____

_____

_____

_____

"Remind yourself to make it fun. That business. That sport. That relationship. Remind yourself to make it fun."

In Pen:

_____

_____

_____

_____

_____

In Pencil:

_____

_____

_____

_____

_____

"That work today, won't show until tomorrow. Just keep going."

In Pen:

_____

_____

_____

_____

In Pencil:

_____

_____

_____

_____

"It's challenging to become great, stay great, or remain great on your own."

In Pen:

_____

_____

_____

_____

_____

In Pencil:

_____

_____

_____

_____

_____

"It's disrespectful to give an opponent or competitor only 75 percent of your effort."

In Pen:

_____

_____

_____

_____

_____

In Pencil:

_____

_____

_____

_____

_____

"If you're not working on your game of life every day, then you're looking to get leap-frogged by those around you, putting in work, consistently."

In Pen:

_____

_____

_____

_____

In Pencil:

_____

_____

_____

_____

"To become the best we can be,
we should have a relationship
with the work. After a little while,
it'll no longer be work."

In Pen:

_____

_____

_____

_____

In Pencil:

_____

_____

_____

_____

"Action is the loudest voice..."

In Pen:

_____

_____

_____

_____

_____

In Pencil:

_____

_____

_____

_____

_____

"Consistent effort is the staple of greatness."

In Pen:

_____

_____

_____

_____

In Pencil:

_____

_____

_____

_____

Your Confidence is worth investing in.

— CHRIS P AUSTIN —